How to Worry Friends and Inconvenience People

Leila Johnston

snowbooks

Proudly Published by Snowbooks in 2007

1

Snowbooks Ltd.
120 Pentonville Road
London
N1 9JN
Tel: 0207 837 6482
Fax: 0207 837 6348
email: info@snowbooks.com
www.snowbooks.com

British Library Cataloguing in Publication Data
A catalogue record for this book is available from the British Library. Remember: library books should always be
returned with more words in than when they were borrowed.

Printed and bound by J. H. Haynes & Co. Ltd., Sparkford

ISBN13 978-1-905005-7-58

How to Worry Friends
and Inconvenience People

Leila Johnston

About the author

Leila Johnston is the founder of
www.worryfriends.com.
She lives in Elstree where she spends her time
flicking through newspapers and rubbing out any
faces she disagrees with.

> "A table, a chair, a bowl of fruit and a violin; what else does a man need to be happy?" – Albert Einstein

> "A telly." – Leila Johnston

Two moments came together to really kick off this book. The first occurred a few years ago, when my brother gave me a beautiful leather-bound journal. "Think of it like a blog," he said, "but on paper!" Despite the subtle suggestion that I was so involved with the internet I might have lost touch with reality, I did wonder whether he might be onto something. (It is too early to say whether he actually was.) Why not write a diary, then share it with the world without resorting to the internet? You could start small – just whip it out of your pocket at the pub and treat your friends to the bits you're most proud of. Then one day you could 'go public' and share it with literally everyone you speak to. You could even hand your work colleagues a pen and ask them to add their thoughts (you'll secretly call them 'comments') under each entry. Some might write things they'd like to advertise, like C1aLi5. Some might write simply, "First!" Eventually you'd start a real craze. One day it could even get you fired. The internet makes life simple and convenient – and who wants that? Let's take the long, annoying, often impossible route instead, I thought. Yes. That would be best.

The second formative moment was when, as a student, I decided to kill some of my valueless time by making one of those "29 things to do before you're 30" lists on a website. But somehow the nearer I got to 30, the less amusing the overall idea seemed to become. Soon there was so much material that another home had to be found, and before long my friends were coming on board with excellent contributions of their own. A mere four years later we got around to revamping the site, and it's fair to say that it caught the eye of the world. Worryfriends.com had become an internet phenomenon, endorsed by The Times, NTK, Yahoo!, and literally *some* other websites and blogs. The people of England went crazy for it. There were even calls for me to be your new leader. I'm sure you remember.

When we started inviting public contributions it became clear that everyone has an inner mischief-maker. Most of us know, deep down, that the world could be improved with some good-natured anarchy: we're just too inhibited to make good on our ideas. But let's try to put that shyness behind us, and, for a minute, stop being so bloody British about everything. Have a go at some of the more possible suggestions contained on the pages that follow, and, if you feel unsure, don't despair. Remember: everyone gets self-conscious sometimes. Especially if you stare at them for long enough.

How to Worry Friends and Inconvenience People:

Some Ideas

Say nothing when you answer your phone. They rang you. They can speak first.

If you're moving house, make sure you do everything before you go. Remember to write "beware" in big red letters on the wall, then loosely paper over it.

Look through a different person's window on each day of advent.

Stick up a photo of your sweetheart in your swimming pool locker door.

Instead of using smileys, take pictures of your own face in different expressions and upload them.

Ask for sandwich fillings while pointing at other ones.

☞

Instead of having a day out at a stately home, visit a show home. It's free.

Buy a trolley for £1 at your local supermarket.

Instead of using the fancy "zoom" on an online map, just hold a normal map very close to your face.

Instead of having children and contributing to the over-population of the world, audition for an apprentice to replace you.

Get something unexpected pierced, like an eye-bag or the end of your nose.

Line up the horizons of any adjacent landscape
images you encounter.

Begin an exam question, "Ooh, I was hoping you'd ask that."

A

Live your life in alphabetical order.

A B C D E F G
H I J K L M
N O P Q R S T
U V W X Y Z

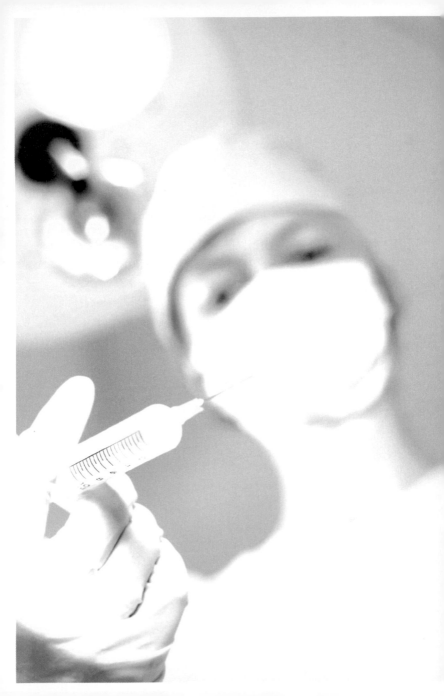

If they ask you to count back from 10 when you're going under anaesthetic, do it really fast — "tennineeightsevensixfivefourthreetwoone." Then you've won.

At the gym, fall into step with the person on the treadmill next to you. It's like being on a road to nowhere with a complete stranger.

Phone a restaurant to book a table, and discretely mention that you're planning to propose to your partner during the meal.

Whenever you see a burnt-out car, frustratedly try to unlock the door.

Help the disabled. Train a speaking dog for the dumb.

Get in behind someone on a revolving door.

When the Post Office clerk asks you where the parcel's going, don't fall for it. They only need to know the name.

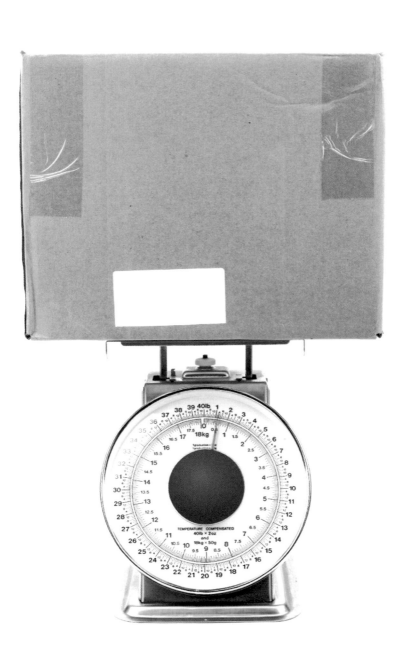

Help yourself to one of those free dogs that people leave outside shops.

Be a volunteer ticket inspector. Walk up and down the aisle, in uniform, asking to see everyone's tickets and scribbling on them.

Send a valentine's card to someone who has recently interviewed you for a job.

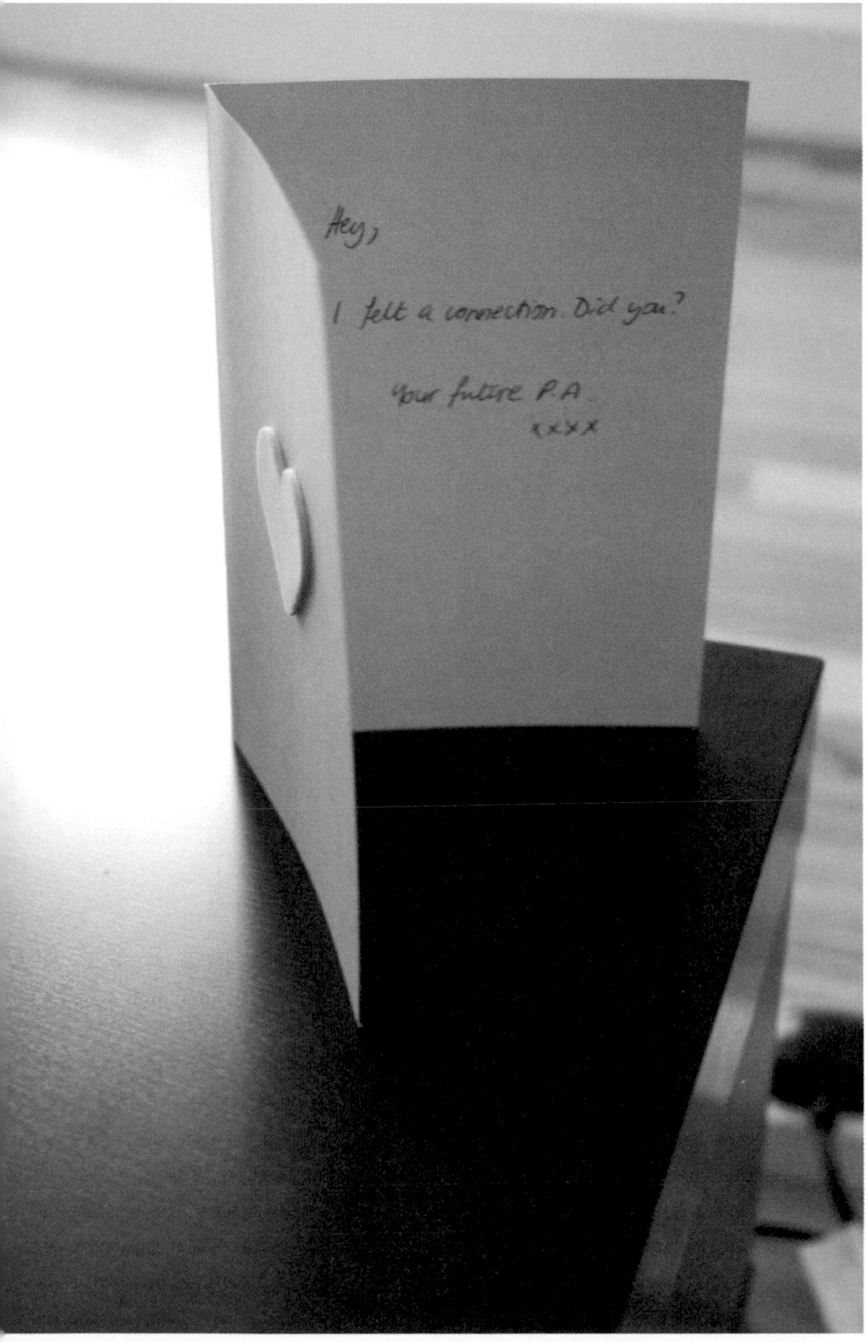
Hey,
I felt a connection. Did you?
Your future P.A
xxxx

Never accept compilation tapes from friends. You'll be left wondering whether they have terrible taste, or just think that you do.

Sit next to the only other person on an otherwise empty bus.

Get on a bus on a hot day and ask the driver if he's got any Callippos.

Impress a future employer at an interview, by demonstrating how well you can ride an imaginary horse.

Attempt "predictive speech" by guessing what people are about to say, based on the first syllable.

If you miss the bin men, it's sometimes OK to just leave your rubbish bags outside charity shops.

Train to be a mystery office worker. Choose an office at random, find a free desk, and work all day.

Take the kids to see the changing of the traffic lights outside Buckingham Palace.

Address a letter to a pillar box.

Make a tea colour chart for the office. Colleagues can write their initials next to the shade of beige they want their drink.

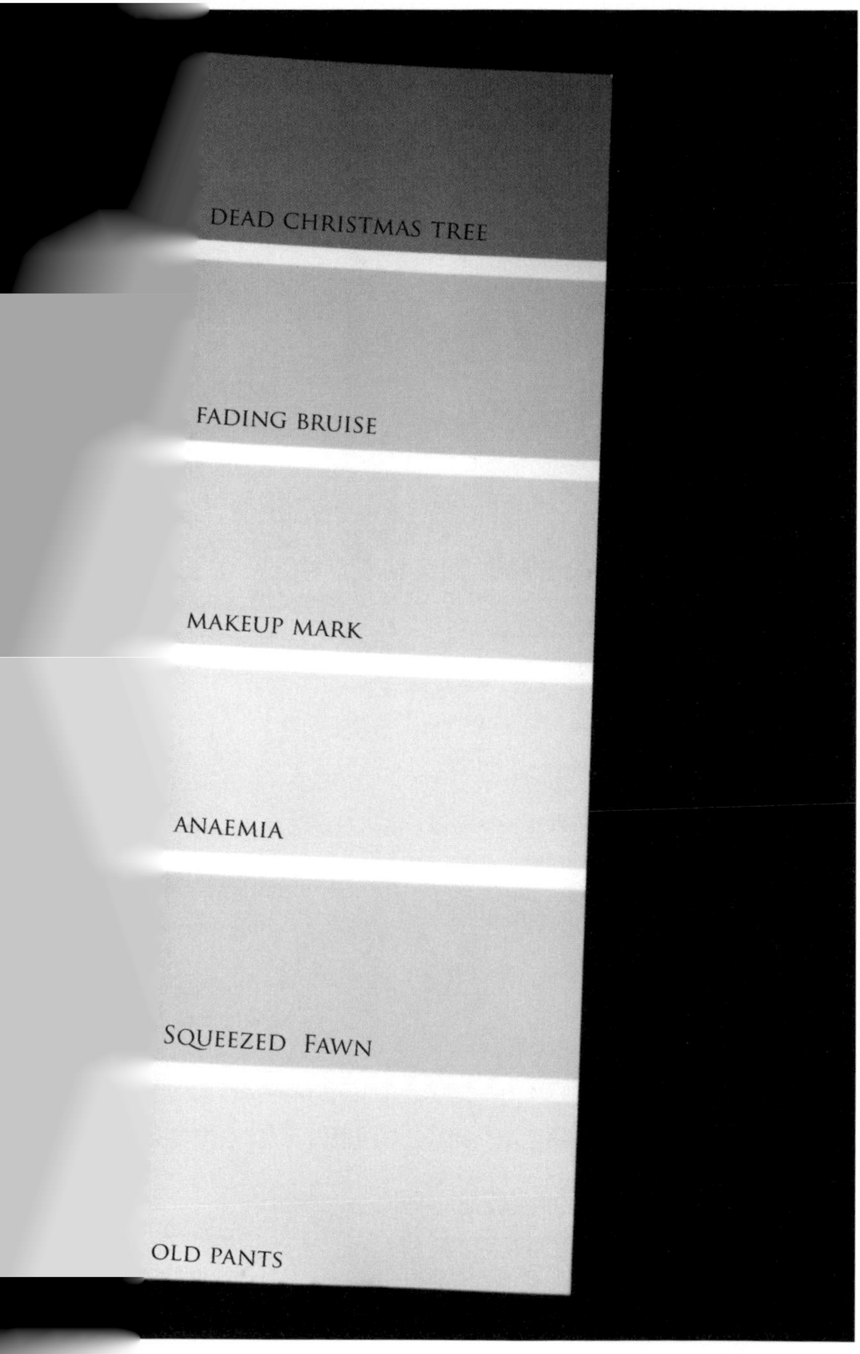

DEAD CHRISTMAS TREE

FADING BRUISE

MAKEUP MARK

ANAEMIA

SQUEEZED FAWN

OLD PANTS

Imagine being followed by the hash key.

Zig-zag down the escalators like you're on the moving walkway in a musical.

Put your Oyster card in a sandwich, and scan that.

Go to a wedding — dressed as a bride.

Use the first page of your chequebook to write a thank you note to the bank. It's only polite.

Get 'known to the police' for good things, like handing in keys regularly or getting your valuables tagged.

Ask the hotel staff if you can put the twin beds together. Then put them end to end and lie across the gap.

Use the comments section of someone else's blog to begin your own parasitic meta-blog.

Leave your comment

Well, here we are, my first blog post on this, someone else's blog. I've had a nice day so far. I can't say much has happened. Here are some photos of my cats:

You can use some HTML tags, such as <b>, <i>, <a>

Choose an identity

⦿ Google/Blogger   ○ Other   ○ Anonymous

Sign in with your Google Account

USERNAME [   ]

PASSWORD [   ]

No **Google** Account? Sign up here.
You can also use your **Blogger** account.

[PUBLISH YOUR COMMENT]   [PREVIEW]

Play Where's Wally on the tube, instead of doing Sudoku.

?

Instead of doing "air quotes," mime asterisks with your fingers for emphasis.

To find out where your spam came from, type 1471
in the subject line and hit reply.

RE: You pay We ship, NoPrescription, CialisPhe

Message   Insert   Options   Format Text

Paste

Clipboa...   Basic Text   Address Check   Att
Book Names   Fi
Names

This message will be sent via Microsoft Exchange Server.

From...
Send   To...   ewuc39uvymr@fonterra.com
Account ▾   Cc...

Subject: 1471

From: ewuc39uvymr@fonterra.com [mailto:ewuc39uvymr@fonterra.com]
Sent: 18 June 2007 13:31
To: MyEmail@internet.com
Subject: You pay We ship, NoPrescription, CialisPhentemineXanaViagraValiun

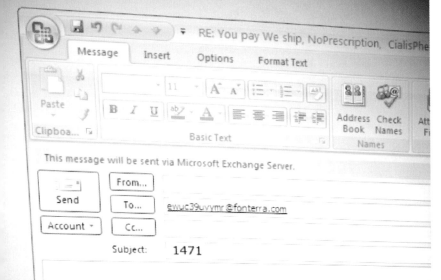

Assume every shop is a family business, and use the staff name tags to make personal enquiries about the team. "How's young Sally Sainsbury doing?" "Could I talk to Mr Woolworth Senior? Is he well?"

If you wake up one day to find yourself surrounded by cardboard boxes and alcohol, don't despair. Pretend you're not homeless — you've just moved in!

Misunderstand the property market and try to sell a house you don't own to an estate agent.

When the "spooky" man comes out on the ghost train, take a flash photo in his face.

If you don't have a candle, show your respects for Diana by sombrely lighting a gas ring.

If your side's losing at the cricket, just clap a bit slower than everyone else to introduce a note of sarcasm into the applause.

Make a website where the links work like a thumbnail, and take you to a giant image of the words.

Take insulin as a recreational drug.

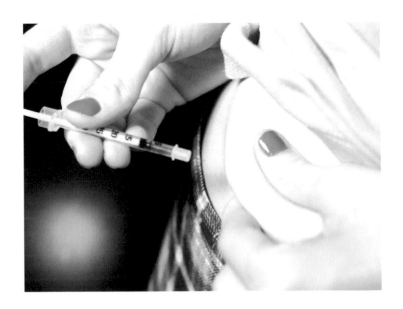

Break up with someone by writing it as the answer to crossword clues.

Sometimes, this works. (You'll need a stamp, though.
The GPO are good, but they're not magic.)

Treat all children in pushchairs as if they are disabled, and with genuine concern ask their parents what's wrong with them.

Plant the seeds of weeds in your enemy's allotment.

Google the words "magic pass1" and your computer will automatically access the google head office. You can finally see what *they're* looking up!

Draw the person opposite you on the train. When you get off, pass them your picture.

When cars stop for you at a zebra crossing, run up and pat their bonnets to show your appreciation.

Say your mobile phone number when you answer it.

If you ever meet Elijah Wood, ask him to do that little tap dance. He loves it.

If you are fourteen, and into the supernatural, why not spell your name like this: "fortean."

Step out of a portaloo and ask the first person you see what year it is.

When singing in church, imagine that god responds to volume — and attempt to drown out those around you to win his favour.

Don't trust the name on the display on the front of a bus – it's sometimes hired out as advertising space by town councils.

Instead of flashing your lights, like everyone else, use your windscreen wipers to "wave" to drivers who let you out.

Try "real life interpretation." Analyse external events as if they are expressions of your subconscious desires.

Empty the contents of a minibar, then replace it all with Tesco's own brand.

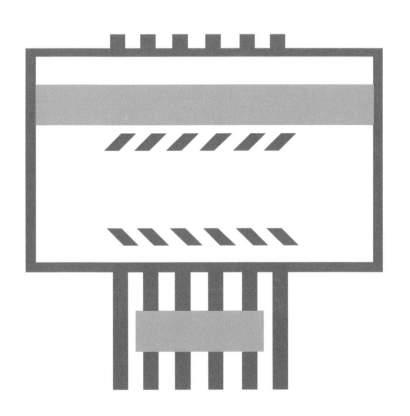

Keep Britain Tidy. Take your shoes off before you leave the house.

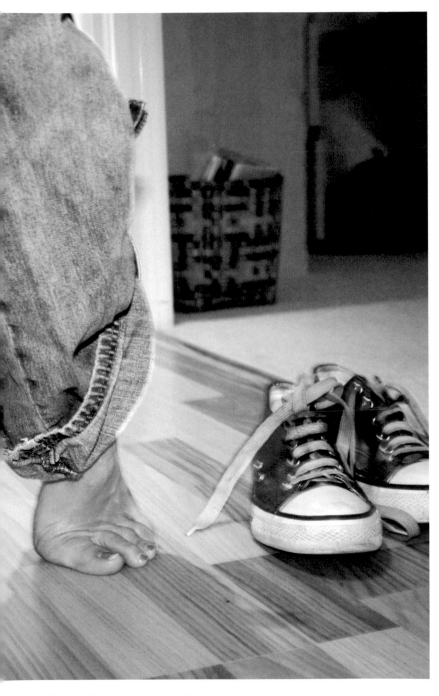

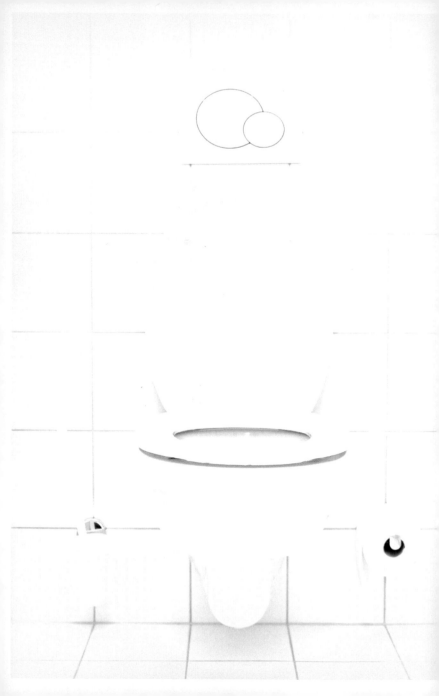

Use "tracing paper" toilet paper to trace your bottom. Then give the picture to the lavatory attendant on the way out.

Use a children's card-making kit to design someone
an original sympathy card.

Lessons of the web: myspace.

Throw a dinner party for your 8 best friends, then set up a seating arrangement to "order" them according to how much you like them.

Put your chair up on the desk before you leave the office.

Show an old person a photo of yourself on a computer screen. And tell them you're on telly.

Give someone a diary for Christmas...that's already been filled in.

4. Pretty day. Ironed. Sewing. St—
ome ace day. Cold late in p.m
—ly windy at night. Stayed at
—'s ace night. Mother & Dad in Fr—

5 Beautiful day Washed my—
—t to see So. Rag about Baby's fe—
—e p.m. too went to see Norma Tal—
— Lady" at night. Good. Baby pee—
— Rummage sale for Church. Bea—
— Whole state horrified. Seven.
—ing cold. Sewing.

—] Going to Mrs. Mallett's for br—
—m. Baby at Mother's. Beautiful
— Going to Fashion Show in eve—
— Mother. Enjoyed it. Quite lon—
8 Busy. Cleaning house
—p & meat from Mom. Town.
— folks to Oakland for day.
—nning. Good. Sleepy.

Dress in your best clothes to go on the motorway.

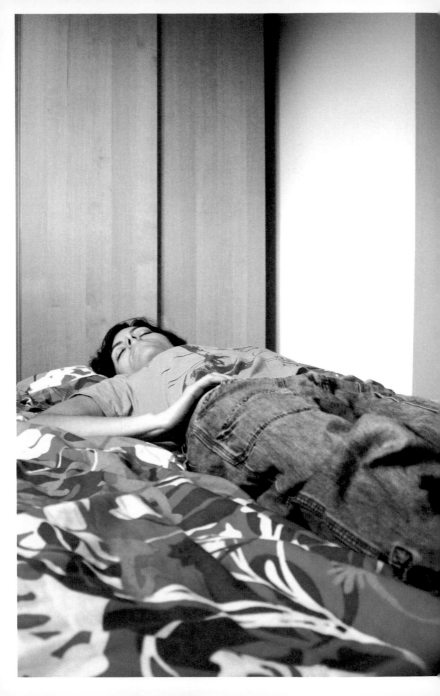

When viewing a house to buy, it's a good idea to try out the beds.

Paint a white line down the middle of a country road.

Just as they finish working on your teeth, it's polite to kiss your dentist gently on the hand.

And always swallow the pink mouthwash liquid the dentist gives you. It's very rude to spit it out.

Go "Blackberrying". Venture out in rush hour and pluck PDAs out of the pockets of office workers.

Lessons of the web: Flickr.

Draw "notes" on photographs in the family album.

Offer someone a crisp, then carefully choose one from your packet, and pop it into their mouth.

Say "ouch!" every time the hairdresser snips a bit of your hair off.

Educate your kids about the important things.
Make them a lovely treasure hunt that ends at a pet
cemetery.

It's polite to run a hire car battery right down before you return it.

If you work in a shopping centre and hate your co-workers, give them all fake presents off the mall's Christmas tree. Insist you thought that was what they were there for.

Rather than waiting years to fulfil your dream of swimming with dolphins, just go swimming with snails instead. Hold onto their shell with both hands as they dive through the water.

Lessons of the web: Livejournal.

Read the personal diary of a friend of someone you
know and write comments under each entry.

Let email conventions inspire you. Answer a letter on the same bit of paper it was sent on, writing your response underneath.

13 Fitzroy Street
Cambridge
Cambridgeshire
CB1 1ER
Tel 01223 305241
Fax 01223 305242
Specsavers Online:
www.specsavers.co.uk/
cambridgefitzroystreet

6th July 2007

Miss L Johnston

Dear Miss Johnston

According to our records, your direct debit for your contact lenses with us has recently been cancelled. I am just writing to check with you that this is correct, and to let you know that a payment is outstanding for contact lenses you have already received.

People cancel direct debits for a variety of reasons, and in some situations, we may be able to offer you an alternative. We very much value you as a customer and will be glad to do what we can to help.

If you have had problems with your contact lenses
Please contact our store (if you have not already done so) if you have been having problems wearing your contact lenses. A member of our contact lens team will be glad to help or advise you.

If you have more contact lenses and solutions than you currently need, or are not completely happy with your contact lens scheme, please discuss it with one of the team. We may be able to offer you a payment 'holiday' while you use the lenses you already have, or an alternative scheme, or different contact lenses that are more suitable for your lifestyle.

If the direct debit has been cancelled by mistake
If you would like to stay on your contact lens replacement scheme , please contact us within the next 14 days to set up a new direct debit.

If you still want to cancel the scheme
You received your last pack of contact lenses in June 07 and your last direct debit payment was collected in May 07 leaving an outstanding balance of £30.00. Please pay this outstanding amount within the next 28 days.*

Thank you for being a customer of Specsavers Opticians - I look forward to hearing from you soon.

Yours sincerely

Louise Brennand
Contact Lens Manager

*Payment can be made with a debit or credit card over the telephone, or in store.

Registered Company
Cambridge Fitzroy Street
Vivoptus Limited
VAT No. 742 2580 50
Registered in England
No. 3078256
Registered Office
2nd Floor, Mitchell House,
Southampton Road, Eastleigh,
Hampshire SO50 9HJ
Directors
J H Churchill
S J Stanray
Specsavers Optical Group
Limited
M L Perkins FBOA

Dear Louise,
   I hope you are well , I am fine. What happens in 28 days and does it involve zombies ? Write soon.
            Your pal, Leila x x x P.S. Do you still love me

Lessons of the web: Amazon.

Criticise all the things you've bought and rate the quality of the people who sell you things in shops.

Lessons from the web: spam.

Tell random people you work for their bank and ask them for their account number.

Actually try to make an omelette without breaking eggs.

When lending money to a friend, write down the serial number of the note so you know you'll get it back.

Lessons of the web: noticeboards.

"Moderate" messages on public pinboards by tearing down any you don't approve of.

Lessons of the web: Amazon.

Instead of flicking through entire magazines in shops, only allow yourself to read the contents page.

Actually cut and paste links. Using glue, stick them into letters you mail to people.

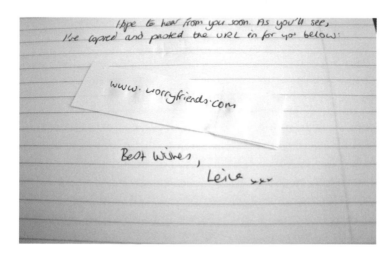

Lessons of the web: homepages.

Make some money by stringing advertising banners across the front of your house.

Always leave some milk in the fridge but never enough for the next person's tea.

Tell your children that before they were born, mummy and daddy used to have three Christmases a year. But now you can only afford one.

Pirate laws apply on fairground pirate ships. Feel free to steal from people seated near you and throw any noisy children overboard.

As a safety measure, always remove your trousers before driving.

Say "life's too short" as justification for menial tasks.
"I'm just popping out to the shops… life's too short."

Draw money out of a cashpoint, then wave it around excitedly shouting "I won!"

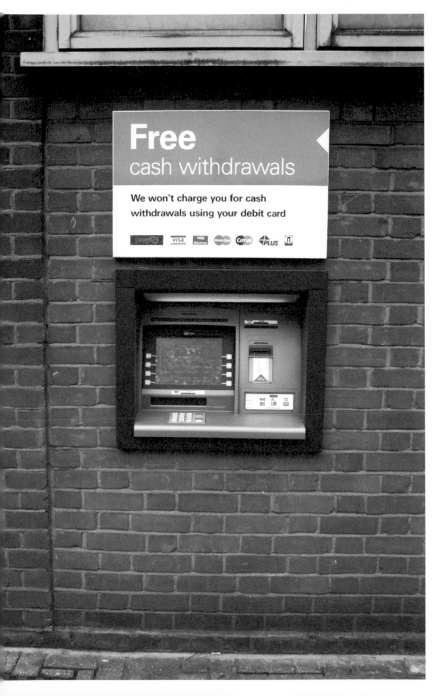

Tell the elderly that if they dial the wheel of an iPod,
they can sometimes get through to the operator.

Tell children the ice cream man has surveillance
equipment in the van and can see if they've been bad.

Make depressing news stories into beautiful blues songs, with "subtitles karaoke."

Ask the taxi driver if he'll put the siren on for you "just for a minute."

Tell children rainbows didn't exist when you were their age, but are an effect of global warming.

Go ⁴⁄₄ing. Remove the wheels of any off-road vehicles you come across in urban areas.

Tell people that Matthew Perry sings the theme tune to Friends.

Only use capitals for the initials of names that you like: James, Rebecca, andi, niki, Matthew, steve.

When the tube train pulls up to your stop, stand up and say, "Well, that's me!" and step off with a matter of fact "thank you driver."

Say "sweet enough already" when offered sugar, and "white enough already" when offered milk.

Tell children that when goats grow up, they become deer.

If you call your TV a gogglebox, try calling your computer a googlebox.

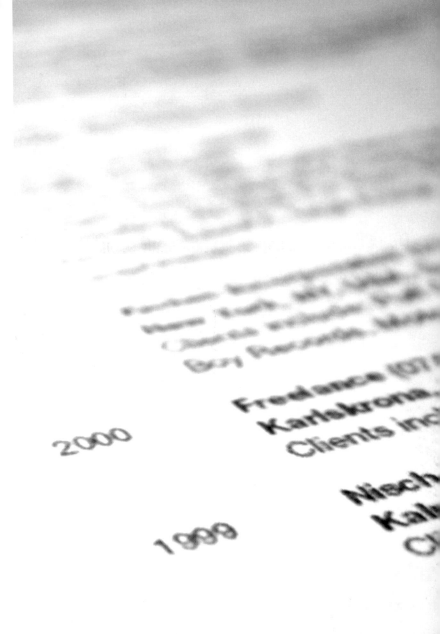

On a CV, it's customary to list how many sexual partners you've had.

Go consecutive house number spotting.

Tell people that sometimes when you buy oysters in a restaurant, there's a pearl in there.

Call a ladder that isn't yours, but belongs to a close relative, a step-ladder.

Insist on pronouncing Scottish names like rappers.
MC Dougal, etc.

Tell children that sand dunes are where they bury old people who die on the beach.

Actually graze on food throughout the day.

Tell people that the main guy in Psycho is Geoffrey Perkins.

Refer to wages lost through 'flu as the "congestion charge."

If questioned, say your favourite superhero is Wickerman.

Tell prospective buyers to be cautious. Sometimes "For Sale" refers only to the sign.

FOR SALE
P&
Palmer & Partners
01206 572233
www.palmerpartners.com
SAXONS
ESTATE AGENTS
01206 517777
www.rightmove.co.uk
106 High Street, Colchester
FOR SALE

Tell children that in the olden days the tube trains used to be better. There were no escalators, but the trains rose to the surface like a sea snake coming up for air, then dipped down again like a rollercoaster.

Insist that Mr Bean was much funnier at the beginning as he was played by Sean Bean.

Tell visitors to the UK that, as a safety measure, British taxis have a handle for winding down the windscreen.

Describe people as "unconventionally ugly".

Say "I've been expecting you," when you answer the door to the postman.

Be more street. Call your flatmates your "flo-mos" and your housemates your "ho-mos."

Refer to white people's dreadlocks as "wedlocks." If you find yourself sitting behind someone with "wedlocks" on the bus, it's traditional to tie them to the hand rail.

Tell children to say "please" and "thank you" to an automatic door.

Try to land a toy helicopter on one of these:

Tell children that your local supermarket is haunted by a Victorian checkout girl.

Tell children that it's lucky to throw coins off a motorway bridge.

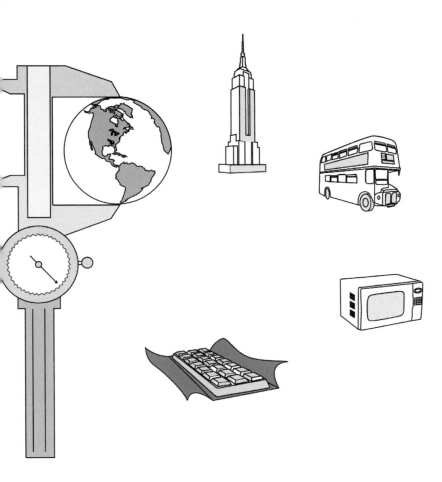

Measure scale and distance in units of chocolate bars, microwaves, Alsatians, double decker buses and empire state buildings.

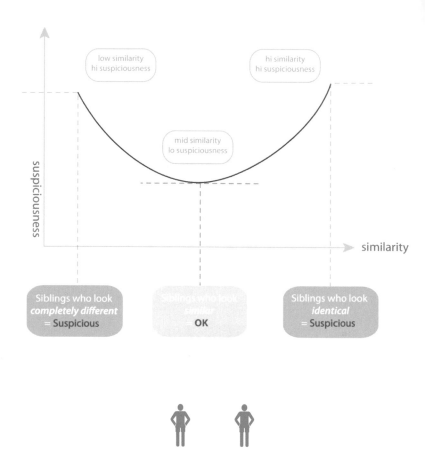

Only completely trust siblings who look a bit similar.

Hide in a car boot for a medium-length journey.

Remember to make air-holes

Space for:
- Flowers
- Cushion
- Thermos
- Crunchie
- Book
- Nightlight
- Whistle

FREE R1DE

Describe an extremely keen swimmer, who takes part in galas and so forth, as a "speedophile."

Describe people who are pointlessly proud of things as "whyumphant."

MOST WHYUMPHANT	
SEXUALITY	BI-CURIOUS (JUST ADMIT IT)
NATIONALITY	MANX
ILLNESS	METABOLIC DISORDERS (THEN - INSOMNIA)
BAND	THE FALL
COMPUTER KEY	$\boxed{\begin{matrix} \pm \\ \S \end{matrix}}$
MEMBER OF U2	THE EDGE (CLOSE ONE)

Look for the face of god in the million dollar homepage.

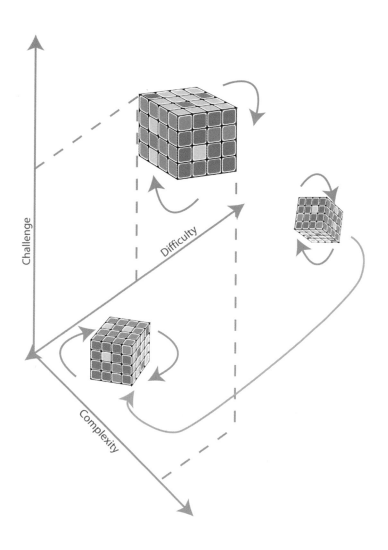

Measure the difficulty of games and puzzles in units of the cubic rube.

As a safety measure, put on 3D glasses before sitting down to your computer, or even at home, watching TV.

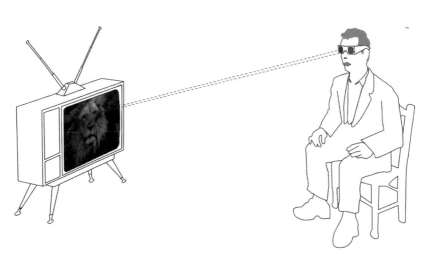

Look for the face of god in a magic eye picture.

Look for the face of god under where it says "do not scratch this off" on a scratch card.

Look for the face of god in the print inside an
envelope from the bank.

New grammar rules #1:

Always put a comma between the two halves of your postcode.

New grammar rules #2:

If you use dots to show a sentence should be read slowly, use a hyphen to indicate speed.

New grammar rules #3:

An upside-down exclamation mark is a symbol of indifference.

Insist you are one of the women in sunglasses in the Friends Reunited photo. Show up to reunions dressed like her.

Put bubblewrap under your doormat to surprise guests.

Create a Bernie Clifton tribute act, with a real ostrich and a fake man.

Describe people going out with far more attractive people as being "20,000 leagues under the sea."

On holiday, ask a stranger to take a photo of you in front of a famous sight. Just as they take the picture, pull a face.

Lessons of the web: wikipedia.

Browse an encyclopedia, writing "citation needed," doing "edits" and adding entries about characters in role player games.

Get the kids to bed early: tell them that if you sleep for more than 8 hours, your brain starts running "repeats" of dreams you had earlier in the night.

Don't bite the hand that feeds you. But do try to touch the hand that gives you your change.

Make a simple Transformers toy for your kids using a pair of stick-on eyes, a packet of chocolate buttons and a mousetrap.

Tell a die-hard UFO nerd that you're skeptical about the existence of weather balloons.

Write a letter of complaint to a company that makes shatterproof rulers. Include this phrase: "rulers were made to be broken."

Thanks to those without whom this could never have happened:

Em Barnes and Rob Jones at Snowbooks

Dave Green and Danny O'Brien at NTK

Tom Stuart

For your support:

Lucy Prebble and everyone who read, liked and contributed to
worryfriends.com

For the jokes you contributed:

Alistair Johnston

Martin Davies

Jake Elliot

Tim Warriner

Ben Moor

Dave Gorman

Rhodri Marsden

Tom Sharp

Joan Franzen